THOMAS KINKADE
Romantic Europe

Harvest House Publishers

Eugene, Oregon

Thomas Kinkade's
Romantic Europe

Text Copyright © 2001 by Media Arts Group, Inc., Morgan Hill, CA 95037
and Harvest House Publishers, Eugene OR 97402
Published by Harvest House Publishers
Eugene, Oregon 97402

Library of Congress Cataloging-in-Publication Data
Kinkade, Thomas, 1958-
    Thomas Kinkade's romantic Europe/ Thomas Kinkade.
       p. cm. — (Chasing the horizon collection)
   ISBN 0-7369-0778-5
   1. Europe—Description and travel. 2. Europe in art. 3. Cities and towns—Europe. I.
   Title: Romantic Europe. II. Title. III. Series.

   D923 .K575 2001
   914.04'55—dc21

2001024435

Media Arts Group, Inc.
900 Lightpost Way
Morgan Hill, CA 95037
1-800-366-3733

Design and production by Koechel Peterson & Associates, Minneapolis, Minnesota

Printed in United States of America

01 02 03 04 05 06 07 08 09 10 / IP / 10 9 8 7 6 5 4 3 2 1

Romantic Europe

My father, now nearly 80, has always been a passionate traveler. When my brother Patrick and I were small, sometimes we wouldn't see Dad for weeks at a time as he headed off for parts unknown. And, as the saying goes, "like father, like son." My brother and I have both inherited Dad's wanderlust. At a moment's notice, we've been known to pack up and hit the road. In my young manhood, I even spent time hoboing my way around America in search of high adventure—and always finding it.

This itch for travel that Dad so kindly passed on to his boys has proved to be a tremendous asset to my work as an artist. Many times during my travels I've marveled at sights I might not have seen had it not been for an innate curiosity that prompted me to take the off-ramp less traveled. Stumbling on the unexpected has resulted in some of my best work. Accordingly, several years ago I devised a small portable "rolling studio" that I take with me on my journeys. Now, within minutes of discovering a must-paint scene, I will have set up my little studio and can be found at work capturing on canvas the magic before me.

That portable studio came in especially handy several years ago when my father, my brother, and I took one of our more memorable trips. Dad, who landed on the beaches of Normandy on D-Day, wanted to go back to the sites he remembered from a half a century earlier. So off we went to Europe—the three Kinkade musketeers.

Along the way, we

stopped here and there, sometimes at a world-famous landmark such as London's Tower Bridge, and sometimes in a small village where I found delights ranging from a small thatched roof cottage to the ruins of an ancient castle. Of course, at such times I immediately sent Patrick and Dad on their way sight-seeing while I set up my portable studio and began to paint.

For most of my professional life as an artist, I've been identified with the unique way I use light. In fact, my reputation as the Painter of Light® rests largely on my use of light to accent my traditional studio paintings—often of cottages, gardens, and nature. But in addition to my popular studio work, I also enjoy employing other artistic techniques, one of which is the impressionistic, "plein air" style done in the outdoor daylight. Artists known for their plein air work include Claude Monet, Auguste Renoir, and Eduoard Manet. The term *plein air* is French and literally means "open air" and, as with all my work, light plays an important part. A plein air painting is done much more quickly than studio paintings—the available light is often fleeting and must be taken advantage of on the spot. Also a plein air artist is more interested in capturing the essence of a place, rather than minute detail.

Can you imagine a better place to capture the essence of than Europe? Not only are there the wonderful cities—London, Paris, Venice, and so many more—but also the small wayside villages, the country roads, the rustic inns, the waterfronts. I'm never at a loss as an artist when I'm traveling through Europe. I always

return home with several freshly painted canvases, often of my plein air work.

For some time we've offered these plein air paintings in our nationwide galleries along with my more traditional work. But now, for the first time, I'm allowing the paintings to be published in book form. For those who have long admired my traditional artwork, I hope you'll be equally pleased with my foray into the world of plein air. For those who will be introduced to the name Thomas Kinkade through my plein air art, I hope your interest will lead you to take a look at the traditional studio art for which I've become known.

Finally, a note about the text accompanying each painting: As I traveled through Europe and painted those scenes that most interested me, I jotted down memories of the day and of the actual painting itself. The smell of bread in Belgium, the World War I soldier in Bloomsbury, the band at Luxembourg Gardens, all added to the sense of place I captured on my canvas. When appropriate I also gleaned information about the history of the site—often learning surprising facts about common European landmarks that I think you'll find interesting.

Come then with me for a brief journey to Europe. Come, let's chase the horizon.

THOMAS KINKADE

Wickworth Cottage

I had just visited Stonehenge and was traveling north across the English countryside when I approached the quaint village of Devizes.

Along the road into town, I noticed a number of charming thatched roof cottages—the kind typically associated with small village English life. I pulled to the side of the road and quickly set up my portable studio and began to paint while the light was good.

I painted quickly, but peacefully. There was a wonderful stillness to the spring afternoon that gave me a surprising sense of expectancy. I almost wished the day wouldn't end. As I worked, I fully expected to see Agatha Christie's Miss Marple walk through the door to attend to her roses or to invite me in for tea and cakes.

This was my first plein air on this trip to England, and it was the perfect beginning. The painting was quickly finished and, pleased with the results, I packed away my portable studio and drove into Devizes where I stopped at the George Inn, a typical British pub. The atmosphere was lively and I could almost imagine C.S. Lewis and his Inklings hoisting a pint amidst discussions about the nature of God.

Like most small English villages, Devizes has a long and interesting history dating back to Dunwallo, a pre-Roman British king. The first Devizes castle was built in 1080 by Osmund, Bishop of Salisbury. In the twelfth century, William the Conqueror's granddaughter, Matilda, gave the village its first royal charter. Then, in 1535 Devizes was visited by Henry VIII and his Queen, Anne Boleyn.

Down through the centuries the village suffered through wars, fires, plagues, and considerable religious controversy. Even the Wesley brothers met trouble in Devizes. When John visited in 1747, the local curate tried to stir up a mob against the preacher. A year later when Charles came to town, he had to escape a similar mob but was attacked by two dogs set upon him and "torn badly."

I, on the other hand, met a much warmer reception. The town was entirely charming and all that a British village should be. Wickworth Cottage near Devizes was the perfect locale for my first plein air of the trip.

Wickworth Cottage

I knew, by the smoke that so gracefully curl'd
Above the green elms, that a cottage was near;
And I said, "If there's peace to be found in the world,
A heart that was humble might hope for it here."

THOMAS MOORE

Yes, there is holy pleasure in thine eye!
The lovely cottage in the guardian nook
Hath stirr'd thee deeply; with its own dear brook,
Its own small pasture, almost its own sky!

WILLIAM WORDSWORTH

Oh give me my lowly thatched cottage again;
The birds singing gaily, that came at my call,
Give me them, and that peace of mind dearer than all.

J. HOWARD PAYNE

Tintern Abbey

The south Wales countryside is full of natural beauty, perhaps nowhere more so than near the small village of Tintern.

Like most people, my first exposure to Tintern Abbey was through the immortal poem by William Wordsworth. It had been during Mr. Purdy's senior English class that I was moved by the poet's ability to put into words the spiritual sense he found in nature. Now I hoped that my abilities as an artist might similarly be affected by that same beauty two hundred years after Wordsworth had seen this view.

I arrived in Tintern on a crisp and clear spring afternoon. The ruins of the abbey were nestled far below the village in the green valley of the Wye River. They seemed larger and more majestic than I had imagined. My impression was that of the physical beauty of nature combining with the spiritual beauty represented by the old abbey resulting in a beauty that could only be described as "ageless."

By late afternoon I had set up my easel at a point high above the abbey. The fading light of day seemed to be the perfect time for this particular setting. The abbey is nearly a thousand years old, founded in 1131 by an order of Cistercian monks. The buildings that remain of the abbey today, however, were built in the thirteenth and fourteenth centuries and are characterized by large Gothic windows and a massive gray exterior that is a tribute to the men who built it to the glory of God seven hundred years ago. I could imagine the activity of the abbey in its earlier years, pulsating with the disciplined life of the religious order of monks.

Tintern Abbey is a beautiful, memorable spot that evokes at one time history, nature, and spirituality. Timeless.

These beauteous forms,
Through a long absence, have not been to me
As is a landscape to a blind man's eye:
But oft, in lonely rooms and mid the din
Of towns and cities, I have owed to them,
In hours of weariness, sensations sweet,
Felt in the blood, and felt along the heart,
And passing even into my purer mind
With tranquil restoration:—feelings too
Of unremembered pleasure; such, perhaps,
As have no slight or trivial influence
On that best portion of a good man's life;
His little, nameless, unremembered acts
Of kindness and love. Nor less, I trust,
To them I may have owed another gift,
Of aspect more sublime; that blessed mood,
In which the burthen of the mystery,
In which the heavy and the weary weight
Of all this unintelligible world
Is lightened:—that serene and blessed mood,
In which the affections gently lead us on...

WILLIAM WORDSWORTH
"Lines Composed a Few Miles Above Tintern Abbey"

Gaze on the Abbey's ruined pile:
Does not the succoring ivy, keeping
Her watch around it, seem to smile,
As o'er a loved one sleeping?

FITZ-GREENE HALLECK

Tintern Abbey

Castles and abbeys have different situations, agreeable to their respective uses. The castle, meant for defence, stands boldly on the hill; the abbey, intended for meditation, is hid in the sequestered vale. Such is the situation of Tintern Abbey. It occupies a great eminence in the middle of a circular valley, beautifully screened on all sides by woody hills, through which the river winds its course; and the hills, closing on its entrance and on its exit, leave no room for inclement blasts to enter.

A more pleasing retreat could not easily be found. The woods and glades intermixed; the winding of the river; the variety of the ground; the splendid ruin, contrasted with the objects of nature; and the elegant line formed by the summits of the hills which include the whole, make all together a very enchanting piece of scenery. Every thing around breathes an air so calm and tranquil, so sequestered from the commerce of life, that it is easy to conceive a man of warm imagination, in monkish times, might have been allured by such a scene to become an inhabitant of it.

WILLIAM GILPIN
Observations on the River Wye...
Made in the Summer of the Year 1770

Cashel Rock, Ireland

Sometimes an unexpected turn of events results in an artistic opportunity I wouldn't have otherwise had.

Such is the case with my plein air painting of Cashel Rock. After a brief business visit with a friend in Ireland, I was scheduled to leave for Wales on the morning ferry. As it turned out the ferry company canceled the trip due to rough seas. I would have an extra unplanned day to roam the nearby Irish countryside.

I headed northeast into County Tipperary and, after about an hour's drive, arrived in the village of Cashel, named for the Rock of Cashel, a huge limestone cliff jutting two hundred feet above the surrounding flat terrain.

At the top of the rock sits the ruins of a huge ancient castle, which certainly seemed in keeping with this charming part of the Emerald Isle. The castle was the home of the Munster kings for more than seven hundred years. Very much a castle fortress, the architecture is a mixture of Irish designs, each reflecting the era in which it was added. Rather than giving the appearance of confusion, however, the overall impression is one of grandeur and unity. As with most ancient castles, there are numerous legends and rumors attached to the history of Cashel Rock. Perhaps the most intriguing concerns the baptism of King Aengus by St. Patrick.

The story is told that Patrick, while performing the baptism, pierced the king's foot with his holy staff. The king remained silent, believing the wound was part of the ceremony. At the end of the baptism, St. Patrick noticed what he had done and was profusely apologetic. The king, however, was unmoved and said that he gladly bore the pain, thinking it a small price to pay to become a Christian.

The cross of St. Patrick, a sculpted six-foot block of stone within the castle, commemorates this event and is said to have been the coronation site for all the Munster kings thereafter. It was a silent afternoon, but one that spoke loudly of Irish history and lore. I could almost imagine St. Patrick himself as he preached at Cashel Rock sixteen hundred years ago.

As a result of serendipitous adventures like Cashel Rock, I've learned that canceled ferries and other unanticipated changes in my plans often make for the most memorable paintings.

Ireland's National Anthem

We'll sing song, a soldier's song,
With cheering rousing chorus,
As round our blazing fires we throng,
The starry heavens o'er us;
Impatient for the coming fight,
And as we wait the morning's light,
Here in the silence of the night,
We'll chant a soldier's song.

Chorus:

Soldiers are we
Whose lives are pledged to Ireland;
Some have come
From a land beyond the wave.
Sworn to be free,
No more our ancient sire land
Shall shelter the despot or the slave.
Tonight we man the gap of danger
In Erin's cause, come woe or weal
'Mid cannons' roar and rifles' peal,
We'll chant a soldier's song.

In valley green, on towering crag,
Our fathers fought before us,
And conquered 'neath the same old flag
That's proudly floating o'er us.
We're children of a fighting race,
That never yet has known disgrace,
And as we march, the foe to face,
We'll chant a soldier's song.

Chorus:

Sons of the Gael! Men of the Pale!
The long watched day is breaking;
The serried ranks of Inisfail
Shall set the Tyrant quaking.
Our camp fires now are burning low;
See in the east a silv'ry glow,
Out yonder waits the Saxon foe,
So chant a soldier's song.

I arise today
Through the strength of heaven:
Light of sun,
Radiance of moon,
Splendor of fire,
Speed of lightning,
Swiftness of wind,
Depth of sea,
Stability of earth,
Firmness of rock.

I arise today
Through God's strength to pilot me:
God's might to uphold me,
God's wisdom to guide me,
God's eye to look before me,
God's ear to hear me,
God's word to speak for me,
God's hand to guard me,
God's way to lie before me,
God's shield to protect me,
God's host to save me
From snares of devils,
From temptations of vices,
From everyone who shall wish me ill,
Afar and anear,
Alone and in multitude.

FROM ST. PATRICK'S BREASTPLATE PRAYER

This castle hath a pleasant seat; the air
Nimbly and sweetly recommends itself
Unto our gentle senses.

WILLIAM SHAKESPEARE
Macbeth

Village Castle, Wales

Often when I'm traveling, I like to abandon the main highways and, like Robert Frost, seek out the road less traveled.

One afternoon while driving through the Welsh countryside, I noticed how perfect the light seemed for painting. Yet as I drove along the main highway, nothing seemed to capture my interest enough to stop the car and set up my easel. So, following my instincts, I turned off the main road and drove up into the rolling Welsh hills of Pembrokeshire. I noticed some historic markers pointing ahead toward a township called Parish Llawhaden.

Llawhaden translates roughly as "the land of Aidan." Aidan was the patron saint of an historically important church in the parish and a follower of David, the patron of Wales. Entering the town I was immediately drawn to the ruins of an ancient Welsh castle, Castle Llawhaden. According to legend, the land on which the castle stands had to be won from Satan in a barrel-rolling contest. Archbishop Bernard, an eighth-century clergyman, had bested the devil in the event and Satan, angered at his loss, turned into a snake and abandoned the area, leaving it to the archbishop for the purpose of ministry.

I set up my easel, surrounded by the pastoral beauty of the area. More than five hundred varieties of primroses grow on the castle grounds.

After painting the village castle, I sat in an open tower of the Castle Llawhaden and took in the view from this new vantage point—a view of a lightly descending valley shrouded with a delicate Welsh mist. A gentle breeze was moving peacefully through the grasses, flowers, and trees.

It was a perfect time and place for reflection.

20 HELVETIA

Village Castle, Wales

Why don't we live here always? Always and always.

DYLAN THOMAS
As a boy, on his home Pembrokeshire

Where the gulls go to be lonely.

DYLAN THOMAS
On the coast of Pembrokeshire

Build on, and make thy castles high and fair,
Rising and reaching upward to the skies;
Listen to voices in the upper air,
Nor lose thy simple faith in mysteries.

HENRY WADSWORTH LONGFELLOW

Tower Bridge, London

As scattered clouds passed over the Thames, they cast an ever-changing pattern of light and shadow on Tower Bridge, one of London's many magnificent landmarks.

The shifting sky gave me a succession of changing vistas from which to choose. I picked a quality of light that brought the radiant blue accents into sharpest relief.

Tower Bridge is relatively young compared to the rest of the city—it was completed in 1894 after eight years of construction. Though the river traffic of the Thames has diminished in the past century, the twin bascules still open for river traffic several times a week. For several years there was a walkway open to pedestrians so that they could cross without having to wait for the water traffic to pass. However, so many pedestrians preferred to wait and watch the bascules rise and the boats to pass through, that the walkway was closed for lack of use.

Although the bridge didn't open to allow ships to pass while I painted, I could understand anyone's preference to watching the bridge in action. For even while standing still and regal, the view was beautiful. The bridge a demonstration of man's design, the Thames—the soul of London— a display of God's design.

The Thames nocturne of blue and gold
Changed to a Harmony in grey:
A barge with ochre-coloured hay
Dropt from the wharf: and chill and cold

The yellow fog came creeping down
The bridges, till the houses' walls
Seemed changed to shadows and St. Paul's
Loomed like a bubble o'er the town.

OSCAR WILDE

16

Tower Bridge, London

I have seen the Mississippi. That is muddy water.
I have seen the St. Lawrence. That is crystal water.
But the Thames is liquid history.

JOHN ELLIOT BURNS

Sweet Thames! run softly, till I end my song.

EDMUND SPENSER
Impression Du Matin

Bloomsbury Café, London

I remember with fondness the day I painted this rustic English pub.

I had walked through London's historic Bloomsbury district, renowned for its elegant Georgian Squares—Bedford Square, Bloomsbury Square, and Russell Square—each of which is set around a central park. The nearby shops included antiquarian bookstores and art galleries, increasing my awareness of the rich literary and artistic heritage surrounding me. I could well imagine the many English authors and artists of the past who had walked these streets before me.

As I settled across the street from this charming Bloomsbury pub and began to paint, I was approached by an elderly Englishman. He watched me for a while and, before long, began to tell me of his wartime experiences during "Britain's Finest Hour." Far from being a distraction, this fascinating man and his memories enhanced my sense of Britain itself, and Bloomsbury in particular. This gentleman, though unseen in the resulting canvas, is nonetheless present through his profound influence on me that day.

…to walk alone in London is the greatest rest.
VIRGINIA WOOLF

Oh, to be in England
Now that April's there,
And whoever wakes in England
Sees, some morning, unaware
That the lowest boughs and the brush-wood sheaf
Round the elm-bole are in tiny leaf,
While the chaffinch sings on the orchard bough
In England — now!

ROBERT BROWNING

*I can no more pass through…
Bloomsbury Square without
thinking of [Richard] Steele and
[Mark] Akenside, than I can prefer
brick and mortar to wit and poetry,
or not see a beauty upon it beyond
architecture in the splendour of
the recollection.*

KATE DOUGLAS WIGGIN
Penelope's English Experiences

*One of the surprises of London is
the number of its little parks and
grassy squares. They are found in
the most unexpected places, and
one comes upon them unawares.
Sometimes they are surrounded by
business buildings, and sometimes
walled in with residences. Even the
old churchyards are practically
public gardens, and one may see
men and women sitting on benches
amid tombstones of the dead of
two centuries ago.*

FRANK G. CARPENTER
Carpenter's World Travels, 1926

Piccadilly Circus, London

During my stay in London, I wanted to be sure and visit the West End, particularly Piccadilly Circus.

During the day the area is a bustling, odd-angled intersection, thronged with Londoners and tourists alike. At night the lights blaze brightly, making Piccadilly England's equivalent of New York's Times Square.

The day was a typical rainy London day. But by late afternoon, the rain slackened and the clouds lightened. It would rain again later, but not before I captured the shimmering streets of Piccadilly, filled with shoppers and tourists.

In the middle of Piccadilly Circus stands a landmark statue, a favorite of tourists' cameras. The winged figure is generally thought to be that of romantic Eros.

However, the statue is actually the Angel of Christian Charity, erected in 1893 in honor of Victorian philanthropist Lord Shaftesbury.

Piccadilly Circus, of which you have heard so much, is an irregular circle formed by the meeting of several streets. To the south is the Haymarket; from the east come Shaftesbury Avenue and Coventry Street. Regent Street crosses it from the northwest, and to the west lies the street called Piccadilly. Here, the shopping, theatre, and restaurant sections of London meet, forming a great traffic centre that is thronged both day and night.

FRANK G. CARPENTER
Carpenter's World Travels, 1926

When a man is tired of London, he is tired of life; for there is in London all that life can afford.

SAMUEL JOHNSON
Boswell's Life of Johnson

Piccadilly Circus, London

The room was dim with the light of a single lamp; the rain had ceased; the roar of Piccadilly came to us softened by distance. A belated vendor of lavender came along the sidewalk, and as he stopped under the windows the pungent fragrance of the flowers was wafted up to us with his song.

"Who'll buy my pretty lavender?
    Sweet lavender,
  Who'll buy my pretty lavender?
    Sweet bloomin' lavender."

The tune comes to me laden with odours. Is it not strange that the fragrances of other days steal in upon the senses together with the sights and sounds that gave them birth?

KATE DOUGLAS WIGGIN
Penelope's English Experiences

Biarritz

On this trip through Europe, I stopped to take in the culture of France's Atlantic coast.

Biarritz was once just a sleepy whaling village in the Pays Basque in the southwest of France—until Napoleon III and Empress Eugenie discovered its charm and built a palace on the beach. Since then it's become a popular seaside resort featuring the wonderful French cuisine, beautiful beaches (its Grand Plage attracts surfers from around the world), and one of the oldest and most beautiful golf greens in all of Europe. Royal families frequently have made Biarritz their destination. Queen Victoria came frequently over the course of twenty years.

As I painted this breathtaking scene, the delicious smell of fresh cooked seafood drifted over to me from beneath the brightly colored awnings.

Biarritz combines a sense of modern French cosmopolitan with an old-world sensibility of the Basque fishing village it once was.

I know no place more charming than Biarritz. Nowhere else have I seen old Neptune destroying Cybele with more power, joyousness, and grace. On all this coast there is abundance of noise...

Its friendly people, its pretty white houses, its great dunes, its clean sand, its huge caves, its splendid sea, all make Biarritz a wonderful place.

VICTOR HUGO

Above the principal beaches with its graceful curves of silver sand under the tamarisks, and above the beach of the Basques, lying so pleasantly under the high cliffs, one finds nothing but magnificent villas, palaces, casinos, parks, chapels, churches, aquariums, buildings of all sorts...

ARMAND PRAVIEL
Biarritz Pau and the Basque Country

Thomas Kinkade

Ste. Mere-Eglise

On rare occasions, I find myself painting a scene that has a personal connection.

The day that I painted the small French village of Ste. Mere-Eglise, I had just come from nearby Omaha Beach, where American soldiers had landed on D-Day. My father, who had been part of that historic day, was with me. We had walked that same beach he had walked more than fifty years earlier, and he had movingly recounted his memories of the event. We visited the Normandy Memorials and the vast cemetery with row after row of crosses, each representing the death of men from my father's generation.

We left with a mixed sense of melancholy and respect for what had happened on that day of liberation. We then drove the eight miles to Ste. Mere-Eglise, which had been my father's first official stop on the *Voie de la Liberation*, the Liberty Highway. It was here, in this village, that hundreds of American GI's parachuted into the streets and liberated the town the day after the D-Day invasion. To this day, the village takes pride in its claim to fame as the first French town liberated from the Germans during World War II.

The Musee C-47 is a museum, parachute-shaped of course, that displays a vast array of military hardware that testifies to the not-to-be-forgotten events of World War II. In fact, the war and its aftermath are ever present in this small village all these decades later. Curio shops offer mementos of the occasion, including authentic war memorabilia—canteens, medals, spent shell cases, and much more.

VILLA REGINA

Across from the square is the town church which was established in the eleventh century and expanded over the next several hundred years, taking on much of its present form in the fifteenth century. During the war, the majestic stained-glass windows were destroyed. But they were replaced with elaborate new windows that commemorate the town's liberation. The windows have a worldwide reputation among aficionados of stained-glass art. For those who have seen the movie *The Longest Day*, this church is the site where a soldier, played by Red Buttons in the movie, was stranded as his parachute caught on the church steeple. The soldier hung there through the night, watching the long and vicious battle on the streets below.

Today, typical village life goes on here. Like most small European villages, Ste. Mere-Eglise has a central town square where much of its social and economic life is concentrated. We arrived to the bustle of a local farmer's market and the lively talk of the townspeople exchanging local gossip. The smell of grilling sausages and freshly picked fruits and vegetables filled the air.

We wandered through the village and by late afternoon, when the farmer's market had closed and the townspeople had dwindled to a few, I set up my easel and began to paint. After a while, a boy appeared at my side and, viewing the canvas, he pointed to a small establishment on the painting and said in hesitant English, "My father's shop!"

Because of the personal memories my father shared with me about his presence here as one of the men who liberated Ste. Mere-Eglise, this painting has special meaning to me.

The men of Normandy had faith that what they were doing was right, faith that they fought for all humanity, faith that a just God would grant them mercy on this beachhead or on the next. It was the deep knowledge—and pray God we have not lost it—that there is a profound, moral difference between the use of force for liberation and the use of force for conquest. You were here to liberate, not to conquer, and so you and those others did not doubt your cause. And you were right not to doubt.

PRESIDENT RONALD REAGAN
Omaha Beach
40th Anniversary of the
D-Day Invasion, June 6, 1984

Ste. Mere~Eglise

Full victory—nothing else.

GENERAL DWIGHT D. EISENHOWER
To his troops as they prepared for D-Day

It is not enough for a landscape to be interesting in itself. Eventually there must be a moral and historic interest.

STENDHAL

Chartres

The drive to the French town of Chartres is along a wide sweeping plain, uncharacteristically barren.

An occasional farmhouse breaks the monotony. But then far ahead one sees a fine point of light, starlike, on the horizon. Drawing closer, it seems to be a building, though still indistinct. Two towers and a broad roof gradually come into view, shimmering in the light.

And then, the traveler is struck silent as the majestic cathedral becomes apparent. Words are useless to describe the visual impact.

Later we discover that the cathedral sits atop a small hill rising out of a shallow valley where the town of Chartres is located. That's why it appears so magnificent from afar. That's also why it's been such a popular destination for artists from around the world. It's truly one of the most painted and photographed architectural wonders in the world. But rather than capture its familiar entrance, as so many others have done, I chose to paint the cathedral from a distance and at an uncommon angle. I located on the northeast edge of the town of Chartres on the Rue de la Tannerie and began to paint.

There's something about the glory of an ancient cathedral that draws my heart upwards and reminds me that the faith I hold so dear is part of a legacy stretching backwards into time. Men and women, famous and unknown, lived and died for the truth they found in the grace of God. Some have left their testimony—in writing, in painting, in architecture—that helps light the way for me as I walk my own spiritual path on my own spiritual journey.

He who walks through the meadows of Champagne

At noon in Fall, when leaves like gold appear,

Sees it draw near

Like some great mountain set upon the plain,

From radiant dawn until the close of day,

Nearer it grows

To him who goes

Across the country. When tall towers lay

Their shadowy pall

Upon his way,

He enters, where

The solid stone is hollowed deep by all

Its centuries of beauty and of prayer.

JOYCE KILMER
"The Cathedral"

Chartres

From Paris we paid a visit to Chartres, which contains one of the most magnificent cathedrals in France. Its dimensions are vast, its proportions are elegant, and its painted glass is unequalled. Nothing can be more beautiful than its three rose-windows.

JAMES NASMYTH

This building is like a book. Its architecture is the binding, its text is in the glass and sculpture… If it were a person, it would be a woman, a very dignified old lady. She is beautiful. She is royal. She has kept her charms.

MALCOLM MILLER

Christian faith is a grand cathedral, with divinely pictured windows. Standing without, you can see no glory, nor can imagine any, but standing within every ray of light reveals a harmony of unspeakable splendors.

NATHANIEL HAWTHORNE

Notre Dame, Paris

Historic cities such as Paris offer the artist a multitude of choices.

But for me, the selection of Notre Dame was an easy one. First, I love the grand cathedrals and churches of Europe. The history, the sheer beauty, and the spiritual association appeal to me both as an artist and as a Christian.

To the casual observer, the huge Cathedral of Notre Dame, like many other European cathedrals, is a patchwork of architectural styles. My first impression was to paint it from the front as many others have done. Instead, I did a sketch from the front and then moved to a different vantage point to begin my plein air. I settled on a view of the back of the Cathedral, along the south bank of the Seine.

As sometimes happens, several onlookers gathered to watch me work. After a few minutes one man offered to buy my painting on the spot. I declined, as I always do, with the explanation that I never sell anything without showing it first to my wife, Nanette. I'm always extremely flattered at these offers and usually engage the prospective buyer in conversation.

It is a beautiful and imposing building, whether viewed from the front or rear. It is an inspiring spectacle when this grand old building is filled with eight or ten thousand worshippers, and the vast choir of sweet-voiced women are chanting sacred music in harmony with the thundering tones of the magnificent organ.

RODNEY GLISAN
Two Years in Europe, 1887

...a dazzling sea of roofs, chimneys, streets, bridges, squares, spires, and steeples. Everything burst upon (his) vision, at once,—the carved gable, the steep roof, the turret hanging from the angles of the walls, the eleventh-century stone pyramid, the fifteenth-century slate obelisk, the round bare tower of the donjon-keep, the square elaborately wrought tower of the church, the great, the small, the massive, and the light. The eye wandered for a time, plunging deep down into the labyrinth, where there was no one thing destitute of originality, purpose, genius, and beauty, nothing uninspired by art, from the tiniest house with carved and painted front...

VICTOR HUGO
The Hunchback of Notre Dame

Notre Dame, Paris

...and the great Hall with its blue and gold, its Gothic windows, its statues, its pillars, its immense vaulted rood so profusely carved—and the gilded chamber—and the stone lion kneeling at the door with head abased and tail between its legs, like the lions of Solomon's throne, in that attitude of humility which beseems Strength in the presence of Justice? And the beautiful doors, and the gorgeous-hued windows, and the wrought iron-work which discouraged Biscornette—and the delicate cabinet-work De Hancy? How has time, how has man, served these marvels? What have they given us in exchange for all this...

VICTOR HUGO
Notre Dame de Paris

Paris, St. Michel

Artists can often be seen setting up their easels to capture this famous sight in all its glory.

Crowds habitually gather here to enjoy the majestic architecture and the gorgeous flowers and trees planted round about. Part of the enjoyment is watching the painters bring it all to life on canvas.

Crowds of Parisians gathered to watch as I painted this famed boulevard once frequented by Hemingway. Some of the admirers even paid me the compliment of believing I was a Frenchman.

When I am painting in the great European cities—Paris, London, Venice—I am always cognizant of being surrounded by history. I can set up my easel to paint on a Parisian street, knowing that it is not unlikely that Van Gogh, Renoir, or Calliabotte might have chosen this very spot themselves to undertake one of their masterpieces. And just as they attempted to capture the fleeting moments of splendor that arise in a busy train station, along the pathway of a city park, or as night falls and the electric lights of a café blink on, so I have attempted to capture my own vision of beauty and wonder with the quick strokes of my brush.

If you are lucky enough to have lived in Paris as a young man, then wherever you go for the rest of your life it stays with you, for Paris is a moveable feast.

ERNEST HEMINGWAY

The city was herself again when the rain was over, and so were we. What a change! The fashionable streets, avenues, and boulevards were crowded with gay, well-dressed men and women, from all parts of the world, who seemed to vie with the Parisians themselves in sprightliness and gayety…I have passed across this beautiful Place about a thousand times. I have seen it in the quiet hours of the night, when its solitude was like a wilderness; in the early evening, when brilliantly lighted by gas and electricity; when its lamps, joining those ascending the Champs Elysées, as far as the Triumphal Arch, defined an avenue which seemed to have no end; when its silvery fountains were in an effulgence of glory, and the surrounding groves resonant with vocal and instrumental music.

RODNEY GLISAN
Two Years in Europe, 1887

Paris—a veritable ocean. Take as many soundings in it as you will, you will never know its depth.

PERE GORIOT

Paris, St. Michel

Aside from the bookshops at the place St. Michel, most of the shops up to St. Germain are thread and shoe places, and there are some bookshops on the other side too, behind the construction barrier. Another thing, the street is full of traffic, four lanes of it and the light is coming off windshields too, and there is sort of a haze of fumes: rush hour in early afternoon.

Contrary to what I believed, the Boulevard St. Michel is not an old Paris street, dating as I thought, to Roman times—but a fairly recent assembly, starting in 1859—from the Pont St. Michel up to rue Cujas, and continuing beyond in 1859—and it was first called Sébastopol-Rive-Gauche and only became St. Michel in 1867. It absorbed the part of rue de la Harpe beyond the boulevard St. Germain and disappeared a number of older streets, most of them dating from the 12th century.

Metropole Paris

Luxembourg Gardens

It's hard to imagine a more dramatic history than that of Luxembourg Gardens.

In 1615 Marie de Medici asked her husband, Henri IV, to do her a little favor: build a palace similar to Palazzo Pitti, her childhood home in Florence. The work begins on land acquired from the Duke of Luxembourg. A decade later, the work is finished and Marie's son Louis XIII ascends to the throne upon Henri's death. A mother/son dispute results in Marie's banishment to Cologne, where she dies in poverty. The palace eventually becomes a factory, then a prison, and in 1797, Napoleon Bonaparte appropriates it for the French Senate. The 60-acre gardens stand today as one of the finest in Europe—and have served as the source of inspiration for artists for more than a century.

As I set up my portable studio to paint, a band concert behind me drew a crowd to the gardens, filling the park with music and color. It was a perfect day to be in France.

Everyone, or nearly everyone,…knows the Luxembourg Gardens;…listening to water trickling from a vase that a great stone Neptune held in his arms at the end of the alley, my thoughts embraced not only the garden, but all I know of Paris…

GEORGE MOORE
Memoirs of My Dead Life

Adieu, delightful land of France! O my country so dear, which nourished my infancy! Adieu, France—adieu my beautiful days!

MARY, QUEEN OF SCOTS

Brussels

Often as I paint, I find I'm influenced by all my senses, not just my sight.

On this day in Brussels, the delicious smell of Belgian waffles filled the air as I painted this bustling street scene. That delightful aroma, combined with the overcast weather and the aliveness of the Belgian people as they went about their lives, resulted in a sense of Brussels that I wanted to capture on canvas. If you can sense that aroma, and imagine the movement of the busy Belgians, then I've succeeded beyond all expectations.

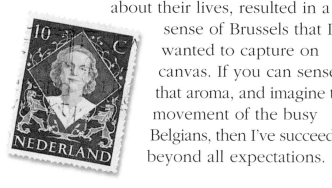

The beauty of spring had tamed and softened these children, these little soldiers of Belgium. They sang, quietly and in parts. Nearly all had bunches of flowers, and I remember the solicitude of one boy over a huge bunch of lilies-of-the-valley which he was carrying.

ETHEL COLQUHOUN
"A Belgian Memory"

The city of Brussels, in its institutions, costume, and manners of its inhabitants, and in its architecture and general appearance is like Paris on a small scale.

RODNEY GLISAN
Two Years in Europe, 1887

*Wars and revolts have left thee little scarred,
And even Progress, the Irreverent,
Spares us the market-place magnificent,
With all its ancient splendor still unmarred.*

*To love thee is a task not overheard—
Thou hast wanton's tender banishment
When Nature's charms with all thy own are blent,
And Spring comes laughing down the boulevard.*

FRANK ROE BATCHELDER
"Brussels"

Heiligenblut

The secluded Austrian town of Heiligenblut ("Holy Blood") sits nestled snuggly amongst the sheltering mountains and is softly covered in a blanket of snow.

The vacant streets suggest that many of the towns-people have found their way home to warm themselves by the fire. The towering mountaintops seem to be watching over this humble town as a silent guardian. The silence of winter and the tranquility in this small valley seemed ageless. I can imagine that many of the residents are descended from Austrians whose lives were not unlike those of these modern day villagers. I can also imagine that these are very close to that area of the Alps where Maria Von Trapp heard the music of the hills so vividly.

Land of mountains...land on river
Land ploughed fields...land of churches
Land of hammer...land of future
Motherland of mighty sons
People blessed with beauty's crown
Austria of proud renown!
Austria of proud renown!

Austrian National Anthem

Hills peep o'er hills, and Alps on Alps arise!

ALEXANDER POPE

Fancy hath flung for me an airy bridge
Across thy long deep Valley, furious Rhone!
Arch that "here" rests upon the granite ridge
Of Monte Rosa—"there" on frailer stone
Of secondary birth, the Jung-frau's cone;
And, from that arch, down-looking on the Vale
The aspect I behold of every zone;
A sea of foliage, tossing with the gale,
Blithe Autumn's purple crown, and Winter's icy mail!

WILLIAM WORDSWORTH

40

Lighting the Way

Salzburg is the home of Wolfgang Amadeus Mozart, and whenever I'm in Austria, I'm reminded of its musical heritage.

Of course, attending a concert is a must. The city has several music conservatories, theatres, and open-air amphitheatres.

Walking through the Old City center, I became more appreciative of the rich Austrian culture, particularly its architecture. The Church of the Holy Trinity was magnificent. But not only is this great city itself wonderful, but also the outlying villages are each unique and charming.

Though we travel the world over to find the beautiful, we must carry it with us or we find it not.

RALPH WALDO EMERSON

When I am…traveling in a carriage, or walking after a good meal, or during the night when I cannot sleep; it is on such occasions that ideas flow best and most abundantly.

WOLFGANG AMADEUS MOZART

Before God and an honest man, I tell you Mozart is the greatest composer ever known in person or by name.

JOSEPH HAYDN

Venice Canal

What can I say about Venice? Venice is a truly magical city, almost unreal in its timeless charm.

I hope I have caught some of this magic in my painting. This painting, which I did as I stood under an awning during a rainstorm, captures the diversity of architecture that adds such interest to the narrow, winding canals of this ancient port city. As you can see from the painting, the color is every bit as delightful on a rainy day as when the sun shines.

Venice is romance. It is a place where time flows as slowly as the waters that meander through the streets of the city. It is a reminder of the beauty that romance brings to our lives when we will allow ourselves to dream, to let ourselves be charmed by all the little wonders that can so easily be passed by unnoticed. Venice reminds us to keep our eyes open...

Those who approach Venice at about sunset on a clear and beautiful May afternoon, as we did at our second visit in 1882, will consider this enchanting city a thing of unsurpassed beauty, a true bride of the sea.

RODNEY GLISAN
Two Years in Europe, 1887

As the sun rose royally behind us, we rode into Venice down a path of gold. O, Venice is a fine city, wherein a rat can wander at his ease and take his pleasure! Or, when weary of wandering, can sit at the edge of the Grand Canal at night, feasting with his friends, when the air is full of music and the sky full of stars, and the lights flash and shimmer on the polished steel prows of the swaying gondolas, packed so that you could walk across the canal on them from side to side! And then the food—do you like shellfish? Well, well, we won't linger over that now.

KENNETH GRAHAME
The Wind in the Willows

Venice, the strongly fortified capital of the province of its own name, a commercial and naval port...its 15,000 houses and palaces, chiefly built on piles, stand on 117 small islands, formed by more than 150 canals, and connected by 378 bridges, most of which are stone. The canals, generally passable by small boats only, sometimes lap the very walls of the houses and are sometimes separated from them by narrow paths. Among these houses extends a labyrinth of lanes, paved with stone, brick, or asphalt, and alive with picturesque and busy throngs.

KARL BAEDEKER
Italy: Handbook for Travelers, 1903

Could any one ever conceive a more appropriate title for Venice that "Queen of the Adriatic"? Like a queen in truth she stands there with her fine palaces, her divine St. Mark's, her striking campanile, in the midst of a group of small islands, her golden domes crowning her and her marble feet kissed gently by the translucent waters of the calm lagoon. Innumerable gondolas and boats with coloured sails pass on, seeming, in their solemnity and composure of movement, like humble suitors approaching the feet of an enchanting queen.

C.T.G. FORMILLI
The Stones of Italy

I spent the late hours either on the water (the moonlight of Venice is famous), or in the splendid square which serves as a vast forecourt to the strange old basilica of Saint Mark. I sat in front of Florian's cafe, eating ices, listening to music, talking with acquaintances: the traveler will remember how the immense cluster of tables and little chairs stretches like a promontory into the smooth lake of the Piazza.

HENRY JAMES
The Aspern Papers

Island Afternoon, Greece

I often choose waterfront scenes to paint.

There's something about calming waves and gentle breezes that I love and that others also seem to be attracted to. This Greek island waterfront seems to offer retreat, relaxation—either sailing on the water or watching lazily from shore.

As I've traveled to seacoasts the world over, that peaceful quality is one that I've noticed everywhere—even where the seas might be rough and wind-tossed—there's still a magnetic pull that brings rest to my soul.

The world is a book and those who do not travel read only one page.

ST. AUGUSTINE

Hear now this fairy legend of old Greece,
As full of freedom, youth, and beauty still,
As the immortal freshness of that grace
Carve for all ages on some Attic frieze.

THOMAS BULLFINCH

So stands the statue that enchants the world,
So bending tries to veil the matchless boast,
The mingled beauties of exulting Greece.

JAMES THOMSON

Thomas
Kinkade

The sea was sapphire colored, and the sky

Burned like a heated opal through the air.

We hoisted sail; the wind was blowing fair

For the blue lands that to the eastward lie...

The flapping of the sail against the mast,

The ripple of the water on the side,

The ripple of the girls' laughter at the stern,

The only sounds:—when 'gan the West to burn,

And a red sun rose upon the seas to ride,

I stood upon the soil of Greece at last!

OSCAR WILDE
"Impression de Voyage"